The Countries

South Korea

Bob Italia

ABDO Publishing Company

visit us at
www.abdopub.com

Published by ABDO Publishing Company, 4940 Viking Drive, Edina, Minnesota 55435.
Copyright © 2003 by Abdo Consulting Group, Inc. International copyrights reserved in
all countries. No part of this book may be reproduced in any form without written
permission from the publisher.

Printed in the United States.

Photo Credits: Corbis
Contributing Editors: Tamara L. Britton, Kristin Van Cleaf, Stephanie Hedlund
Art Direction & Maps: Neil Klinepier

Library of Congress Cataloging-in-Publication Data

Italia, Bob, 1955-
    South Korea / Bob Italia.
        p. cm. -- (The countries)
    Includes index.
    Summary: Presents information on the history, geography, economy, cities, people,
and sports of South Korea.
    ISBN 1-57765-846-9
        1. Korea (South)--Juvenile literature. [1. Korea (South)] I. Title. II. Series.

DS902 .I83 2002
951.95--dc21
                                                                2002018769

Contents

Annyöng hase-yo!

Hello from South Korea! South Korea shares the Korean **peninsula** with North Korea. North Korea has more land than South Korea. But the south has about twice as many people as the north.

South Korea is in southeastern Asia. It has mountains, **plains**, and islands. In the summer, **monsoons** bring much rain.

People lived in what is now Korea at least 30,000 years ago. In the first half of the 1900s, Korea was a Japanese colony. But after **World War II**, the peninsula was divided into northern and southern sections.

In 1950, the north invaded the south and started the **Korean War**, which ended in 1953. Since then, tensions have remained high between the two countries.

Annyöng hase-yo *from South Korea!*

Fast Facts

SEOUL

OFFICIAL NAME: Republic of Korea (Taehan-min'guk)
CAPITAL: Seoul

LAND
- Area: 38,023 square miles (98,480 sq km)
- Mountain Ranges: T'aebaek and Sobaek
- Highest Point: Halla-san 6,398 feet (1,950 m)
- Lowest Point: Sea of Japan (sea level)
- Major Rivers: Naktong River, Han River

PEOPLE
- Population: 47,904,370 (July 2001 est.)
- Major Cities: Seoul, Inchon, Pusan
- Language: Korean
- Religions: Christianity, Buddhism, Confucianism

GOVERNMENT
- Form: Republic
- Head of State: President
- Head of Government: Prime minister
- Legislature: National Assembly
- National Anthem: "Aegug-ga" ("Patriotic Anthem")
- Flag: White with red and blue yin/yang symbol in the center. There are black symbols from the *I Ching* in the corners.
- Independence: August 15, 1945

ECONOMY
- Agricultural Products: Rice, root crops, barley, vegetables; cattle, pigs, chickens, milk, eggs, fish
- Manufactured Products: Electronics, machinery, automobiles, steel, ships, textiles, processed foods
- Money: Won

South Korea's flag

South Korean won

Timeline

2333 B.C.	Tan'gun becomes Korea's king
57 B.C.	Silla, Koguryo, and Paekche kingdoms begin
A.D. 1392	Yi dynasty begins
late 1500s	Japanese invade Korea
1905	Russo-Japanese War ends; Japan controls Korean peninsula
1945	World War II ends; U.S. and Soviet Union occupy Korean peninsula
1948	Southern part of peninsula becomes Republic of Korea; northern part becomes Democratic People's Republic of Korea
1950	Korean War begins when north invades south
1953	Cease-fire divides peninsula into North Korea and South Korea
1981	South Koreans approve new constitution
2000	President Kim Dae Jung wins Nobel Prize

A Nation Divided

About 30,000 years ago, people settled in present-day Korea. They **migrated** from the north and northwest. Some scientists believe that the ancestors of today's Koreans reached the **peninsula** about 5,000 years ago.

According to Korean tradition, Tan'gun founded the country. He became king in 2333 B.C. But historians believe Korea dates from 57 B.C. This is when the kingdoms of Silla (see-lah), Koguryo (koh-goor-yoh), and Paekche (pah-ehk-cheh) began.

In the early thirteenth century A.D., the Mongols conquered Korea. Their empire ruled for more than 100 years. Then in 1392, General Yi (yee) took control. He started the Yi **dynasty**.

The Yi dynasty was the longest in Korean history. During the Yi dynasty, the Korean alphabet, Han-gul (hahn-gool), was created. **Confucianism** (kuhn-FYOO-shuh-NIH-zuhm) replaced **Buddhism** (BOO-dih-zuhm) as the state **ideology**.

In the late sixteenth century, the Japanese invaded Korea. In the seventeenth century, China's Manchu (MAHN-choo) **dynasty** took over. Korea remained part of this empire until the late nineteenth century.

During the late nineteenth and early twentieth centuries, Japan, China, and Russia fought over control of Korea. In 1905, Japan acquired the Korean **peninsula** with a victory in the **Russo-Japanese War**. Japan controlled Korea until the end of **World War II**.

After the war, the United States occupied the southern part of the peninsula. The Soviet Union occupied the northern part. The **United Nations** wanted the Koreans to vote on how to govern their country.

Soldiers in the Russo-Japanese War

Syngman Rhee

The people in the north refused. Those in the south voted to establish the **Republic** of Korea in 1948. The country had a **democratic** government. South Koreans elected Syngman Rhee as the nation's first president.

That same year, people in the north established the Democratic People's Republic of Korea. The country had a **communist** government. Kim Il Sung became its leader.

In 1950, the north invaded the south. This started the **Korean War**. In 1953, both sides agreed to a **cease-fire**. When the fighting stopped, the country was officially divided into North Korea and South Korea.

Kim Il Sung

Park Chung Hee

After the war, South Korea's government and **economy** were unstable. The people blamed President Syngman Rhee for the problems. They removed him from office in 1960.

In a 1961 military **coup** (KOO), General Park Chung Hee became president. The country's economy improved under Park's leadership. He was re-elected three times.

In 1972, South Koreans were upset about the **communist** government in Vietnam. And they were upset at improved relations between the U.S. and China. This led to social unrest.

Park declared **martial law**. He dissolved the National Assembly. A new **constitution** was adopted that gave him unlimited power. It also established an **electoral college**. The electoral college re-elected Park twice more.

Choi Kyu Hah

In 1979, Park was **assassinated**. President Choi Kyu Hah worked to restore order. In 1980, the people elected Chun Doo Hwan president.

In 1981, voters approved a new **constitution**. But the president would still be elected by an **electoral college**. Many people did not like this. So in 1987, the constitution was amended to allow direct election of the president.

In 1988, Roh Tae Woo was elected president. Diplomatic relations were re-established with China and the Soviet Union. In 1993, Roh was replaced by Kim Young Sam.

Roh Tae Woo (R) and Ronald Reagan

Former presidents Chun and Roh were tried for **corruption**. Both were found guilty and sent to prison. Roh's sentence was for 17 years, while Chun's was for life. The men were later **pardoned**.

In 1997, South Korea's **economy** declined. The won decreased in value. And tourism dropped dramatically. In

Kim Young Sam

February 1998, Kim Dae Jung became president. Kim promised to improve relations with North Korea.

Kim Dae Jung

By 1999, the economy had recovered. In December 2000, President Kim Dae Jung won the **Nobel Prize**. The award honored his commitment to **democracy** and human rights in Asia.

The Land

South Korea has three main land regions. They are the Central Mountains, the Southern **Plain**, and the Southwestern Plain.

The Central Mountains region extends throughout most of central and eastern South Korea. It is covered by forested mountains.

The Southern Plain covers South Korea's entire southern coast. It has a series of plains separated by low hills. This is an important agricultural region.

At 325 miles (523 km) long, the Naktong is South Korea's longest river. It flows from the Central Mountains through the Southern Plain. There, the river empties into the Korea Strait.

The Southwestern Plain stretches along South Korea's west coast. It has rolling hills and plains. The Han River flows through this region.

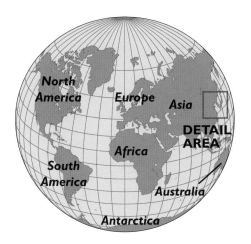

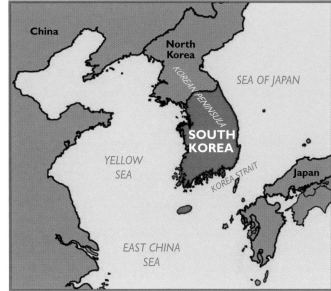

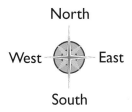

South Korea's land includes many islands. Most are small and unpopulated. But people live on Cheju (CHAY-joo), the largest island. South Korea's highest mountain, Halla-san, is on Cheju Island. It is 6,398 feet (1,950 m) high.

South Korea's climate varies by season. During the summer, the weather is hot and humid. **Monsoons** bring much needed rain. Winters are cold and dry.

South Koreans enjoy a day at the beach on Cheju Island.

Rainfall

AVERAGE YEARLY RAINFALL

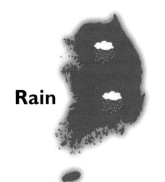

Rain

Inches		*Centimeters*
Under 20		Under 50
20 - 60		50 - 150
Over 60		Over 150

North

West East

South

Temperature

AVERAGE TEMPERATURE

Summer

Fahrenheit		*Celsius*
Over 68°		Over 20°
50° - 68°		10° - 20°
32° - 50°		0° - 10°
14° - 32°		-10° - 0°

Winter

South Koreans

Korean is South Korea's official language. It has about six major dialects. Most Koreans understand all of them.

Han-gul, the Korean alphabet, has 24 letters. South Koreans also use some Chinese symbols in their writing.

Most South Koreans believe in at least some of the principles of **Buddhism**. Almost half of the population is Christian. A few people are **Confucian**.

LANGUAGE

English	Korean
Yes _____	Ne (neh)
No _____	Ani-yo (ahnee-yoh)
Thank you _____	Kamsa hamnida (kahmsah hahmneedah)
Please _____	Chebal (chehbahl)
Hello _____	Annyöng hase-yo (ahnyawng hahseh-yoh)
Good-bye _____	Annyöng-i kase-yo (ahnyawng-ee kahseh-yoh)

Most South Koreans live in cities. Cities have many businesses that provide jobs. They also have more educational opportunities. Better health care is available in cities. And there are more entertainment options.

Housing is another reason most South Koreans live in cities. There are many high-rise apartment buildings and modern houses. But the rapid population increase has forced many people to live in distant suburbs.

High-rise apartment buildings in Seoul

Most South Koreans live in two- or three-story houses made of brick or concrete. Most of these houses have tile or slate roofs. The floors are often covered by oiled papers or mats. Most homes are heated by water pipes in the floors. Almost all South Korean homes have electricity.

A South Korean family at home in the kitchen

Most South Koreans wear Western-style clothing such as that worn in the U.S. or Europe. But they often wear traditional Korean clothing on holidays and

Kimchi

Kimchi is a popular Korean dish.

- 1 large head Chinese cabbage
- 4 green onions
- 1 clove garlic, minced
- 1 dried chili pepper, crushed

- 1 tsp fresh ginger, grated
- 3 tbsp salt

Cut cabbage into 1-inch cubes. Sprinkle 2 tbsp salt on cabbage, mix well, and let stand 15 minutes. Wash cabbage 3 times with cold water. Cut green onions into 1/2-inch pieces, then cut lengthwise into thin strips. Add onions to cabbage with garlic, chili, and ginger. Add 1 tbsp salt and enough water to cover. Mix well, cover, and let stand a few days. Taste each day. When kimchi is fermented enough, cover and refrigerate up to 2 weeks. Makes 1 quart.

AN IMPORTANT NOTE TO THE CHEF: Always have an adult help with the preparation and cooking of food. Never use kitchen utensils or appliances without adult permission and supervision.

special occasions. Women wear long skirts and tight jackets. Men wear baggy pants, shirts, and jackets.

Rice is the most common food in South Korea. The people often eat rice with *kimchi* (KIM-chee). *Kimchi* is a spicy, pickled dish made with Chinese cabbage, onions, and other vegetables. Tea is the traditional drink in South Korea. But coffee is also becoming popular.

Making kimchi

By law, all South Korean children must attend free elementary school through sixth grade. Then, a student may go on to middle school and high school and receive technical training. But parents must pay the tuition. Only qualified high school graduates can attend college.

South Korean students have a picnic in the park.

Making Money

Manufacturing is the most important part of South Korea's **economy**. Clothing, shoes, and **textiles** are the country's main products.

South Korea has a modest supply of natural resources. Miners dig coal, graphite, iron ore, lead, tungsten, and zinc from the land.

Rice is South Korea's most important crop. Oranges are grown on Cheju Island. Farmers also produce fruits, vegetables, and livestock.

South Korea's fishing industry is among the world's leaders. Its fishermen catch filefish, oysters, and pollock.

South Korea burns coal, gas, and **petroleum** in power plants to produce most of its electricity. The country does not have oil reserves, so it must import the petroleum. South Korea also produces electricity with **nuclear** power plants and **hydroelectric** dams.

Growing oranges on Cheju Island

Transportation & Communication

South Korea's railroad system is owned by the government. There is a large subway system in Seoul. A network of highways connects the main cities, where bus and train services are available.

Most people who live in cities own a car. But cars are less common in rural areas. There, bicycles are often used to get around.

Korean Air and Asiana Airlines offer international flights and service between major South Korean cities.

Asiana Airlines

International airports are located in Seoul (SOHL), Pusan (POO-sahn), and Inchon (IN-chahn).

South Korea has many radio and television networks. Many Koreans own televisions, and almost all have radios. About 60 daily newspapers keep South Koreans informed. All are privately owned and published in Seoul.

A South Korean mother and her son buy a newspaper.

Republic of Korea

South Korea is a **republic**. It is ruled by the **constitution** of 1987. It guarantees such rights as freedom of the press and religion. South Korea's people elect the national government leaders. South Korean citizens who are at least 20 years old may vote.

The South Korean president is the head of state. The president is elected by South Korean citizens, and serves a five-year term. The president cannot run for re-election.

South Korea's capitol building in Seoul

The president appoints a **prime minister**, who is the head of government. The president also appoints 15 to 30 State Council members. Each one heads a government department.

The National Assembly is South Korea's **legislature**. It has 299 members. South Korean citizens elect the members of the National Assembly to four-year terms.

Busy Cities

Seoul has a population of more than 10 million people. This makes it South Korea's largest city. It also makes Seoul one of the largest cities in the world. It is South Korea's **cultural**, **economic**, educational, financial, governmental, and political center.

Seoul has many ancient structures. Changdok (chahng-dohk) Palace was built in 1405. There are also modern skyscrapers, such as the 63-story Daehan (deh-hahn) Life Insurance Building.

Downtown Seoul has many marketplaces and shops. Its theaters offer many cultural events. The city's factories produce automobiles, clothing, electronics, iron and steel, radios, and televisions.

Pusan is the second-largest city in South Korea. As the country's major port, Pusan is also the center of South Korea's fishing industry. Pusan's many factories make chemicals, electric and electronic equipment, machinery, plywood, rubber goods, ships, and **textiles**. South Koreans come to Pusan to enjoy its beaches and hot springs. The area is also popular for its religious landmarks.

Seoul's skyline

Celebrations

South Korea's national holidays often mix the past and the present. This makes them popular with people young and old.

South Koreans observe their holidays in a variety of ways. Festival days in the countryside are observed according to traditional **customs**. In the cities, many people combine these traditional holiday customs with parties and family greetings.

Chusok (choo-sohk) is South Korea's day for giving thanks. It is the country's most important national holiday. People visit family tombs and present food offerings to their ancestors.

South Koreans celebrate *sul* (sool) on the first day of the Lunar year. This new year's celebration is the country's second most important national holiday. On *sul*, families conduct ceremonies to honor their ancestors.

Celebrating Confucius's birthday

Many festivals are celebrated nationally. Others are local. They highlight the heritage of a region, city, or village.

The National Folk Arts Competition is a major autumn event. Each year, teams gather at a different time and place. They perform farmers' dances, mask dances, folk rituals, and traditional games.

Events include *ch'ajonnori* (chah-joh-noh-ree), a war game that celebrates the defeat of Paekche forces that tried to invade Silla. There is also a chariot battle, stone-throwing and torch-hurling battles, and tug-of-war.

Sokchonje (sohk-chohn-jeh) is observed twice a year, usually in March and September. It is one of Seoul's major **Confucian** rites. It honors Chinese and Korean Confucian **sages**. A traditional court orchestra performs and ceremonies are conducted by officials in full costume.

Traditional Confucian musicians

Sports & Leisure

South Koreans enjoy a variety of sports, including baseball, tennis, boxing, golf, soccer, table tennis, and wrestling. Martial arts such as judo and tae kwon do are also popular. The traditional wrestling style, called *ssirum* (seer-oom), is a national sport.

Sporting events are often broadcast on television and radio. Each year, the National Sports Festival is held across the country.

Theaters are found in all South Korean cities. There, Koreans can see motion pictures, plays, and concerts. At home, South Koreans enjoy watching television.

Architecture has played an important part in South Korean **culture**. Throughout the country, old palaces, **Buddhist** temples, stone tombs, and Buddhist **pagodas** can be seen.

South Koreans still perform folk dances and music at ceremonies and festivals. The National Classical Music Institute has been preserving folk music since 1954. The Korean National Symphony Orchestra and the Seoul Symphony Orchestra are famous for their performances of Western music.

The National Museum in Seoul

Glossary

architecture - the art of planning and designing buildings.

assassinate - to murder an important person, usually for political reasons.

Buddhism - a religion that was started in India by Buddha. It teaches that pain and evil are caused by desire. If people have no desire they will achieve a state of happiness called nirvana.

cease-fire - a suspension of hostile activities.

communism - a social and economic system in which everything is owned by the government and given to the people as needed.

Confucianism - of or relating to the Chinese philosopher Confucius or his teachings or followers.

constitution - the laws that govern a country.

corrupt - to be influenced by other people to be dishonest.

coup - a sudden overthrow of an established government.

culture - the customs, arts, and tools of a nation or people at a certain time.

custom - an accepted social habit or behavior of a group.

democracy - a governmental system in which the people vote on how to run the country.

dynasty - a series of rulers who belong to the same family.

economy - the way a nation uses its money, goods, and natural resources.

electoral college - a group that elects a president by casting electoral votes.

hydroelectricity - electricity produced by water-powered generators.

ideology - the beliefs, ideas, and doctrines that are held by the members of a group.

Korean War - 1950 to 1953. A war between North and South Korea. The United States government sent help to South Korea. China and the Soviet Union sent help to North Korea. A cease-fire was declared in 1953.

legislature - the branch of a government that makes laws.

martial law - military control of law enforcement at a time when civilian law enforcement agencies are unable to maintain public order and safety.

migrate - to move from one place to settle in another.

monsoon - a seasonal wind that often brings heavy rains.

Nobel Prize - an award for someone who has made outstanding achievements in his or her field of study.

nuclear - of or relating to atomic energy.

pagoda - an Asian temple or tower that is several stories tall. Often, the roof of each story projects from the building and curves upward.

pardon - to forgive anything illegal that a person has done.

peninsula - land that sticks out into water and is connected to a larger land mass.

petroleum - a thick, yellowish-black oil. It is the source of gasoline.

plain - a flat stretch of land.

prime minister - the highest-ranked member of some governments.

republic - a form of government in which authority rests with voting citizens and is carried out by elected officials such as a parliament.

Russo-Japanese War - 1904 to 1905. A war between Russia and Japan for control of Korea and Manchuria. The war ended with the Treaty of Portsmouth.

sage - a person who is very wise, usually an older person.

textile - of or having to do with the designing, manufacturing, or producing of woven fabric.

United Nations - a group of nations formed in 1945. Its goals are peace, human rights, security, and social and economic development.

World War II - 1939 to 1945. The United States, France, Great Britain, the Soviet Union, and their allies were on one side. Germany, Italy, Japan, and their allies were on the other side. The war began when Germany invaded Poland.

Web Sites

Would you like to learn more about South Korea? Please visit **www.abdopub.com** to find up-to-date Web site links about the country and its people. These links are routinely monitored and updated to provide the most current information available.

Index